//////////////////////////////

POEMS FOR OTHER PEOPLE'S LOVERS

//////////////////////////////

by Typewriter Troubadour

Poems For Other People's Lovers
by Typewriter Troubadour

The poems featured in this collection were
written by Jeremy M. Brownlowe under the pen
name, Typewriter Troubadour, between
2015-2021 during his travels of the United
States as a street poet for hire.

ISBN: 978-1-7321765-6-0
Formatting / Artwork by Jeremy M. Brownlowe
Font Face: Remington Noiseless

Typewriter
Troubadour
EST. 2015

POEMS FOR OTHER PEOPLE'S LOVERS

by TYPEWRITER TROUBADOUR

Author's Note:

Being a street poet is an interesting life. I get to travel the country and post up with my typewriter on random street corners to write for curious strangers. About anything.

One of the topics I get a lot is...

You guessed it —— Love!

But Wait, I might say.

Don't think you're getting off that easy!

What type of love are we talking about?

Just like the people who approach me for a poem, love shows up in a myriad of ways.

Love for family. Love for friends. Perhaps to encapsulate the essence of a new relationship or a new crush. There's universal love, there's eros-induced love, or maybe a love poem written to remind you how lovable and badass YOU are. But let's not forget the shadow side of love. The Lost Love. The Longing. Odes to the dearly departed or the ones who got away.

This collection is inspired by all the love wandering muses of America brought to my typewriter table, seeking a reflection of what they felt in their hearts but didn't have the words to say. —JMB/TT

PART ONE:

THE BELOVED

POEMS FOR OTHER PEOPLE'S LOVERS

Our first stop in
Love Land, is to
celebrate the beloved.
It's always interesting
seeing couples try to
describe each other.
Sometimes the words come
easy, other times it's just
a feeling.

These poems spotlight the
unique people who become
our lovers. Whether it
was written for a gift,
an anniversary or to
celebrate an inside joke,
these poems honor the
people in our lives who
matter most.

```
Great Love
        is like
               Great Jazz
             - the cross stitch
                     of two minds -
                  Brilliant & Original
                     When Conjured
                              on the fly
               It is timeless
                        rooted in history
                                 fleeting
                                 and foundational
                           fluid
                                   yet solid
                           tangled
                                 and boundless
                                         all at once
               Oh - how our insides
                         shake like a song
                               our legs
                           can't help but sway
                       in synchopation
                                 to our thumbs
                                      relaxed
                                           snap
          Like Great Jazz
                    our love is all our own
                       bouncing ideas off
                             the tip of our tongue
                     It is our time,
                       our tempo,
                            a masterpiece
                         of our making
                               moments sustain
                       there are norules
                             only freedom
                                   to express
                       all that is unexpected
                                 in the wild gift  in
                                          of
                       improvised romance


            by jeremy M brownlowe
                  Winter 2015
```

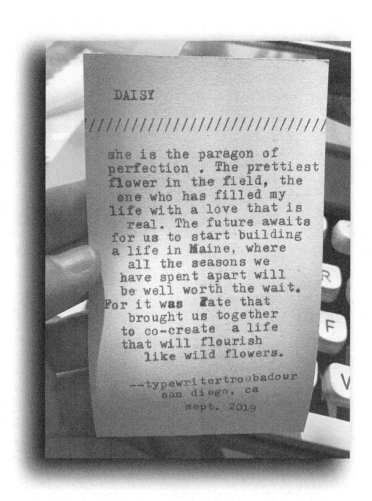

DAISY

///////////////////////////////////

she is the paragon of
perfection . The prettiest
flower in the field, the
one who has filled my
life with a love that is
real. The future awaits
for us to start building
a life in Maine, where
all the seasons we
have spent apart will
be well worth the wait.
For it was Fate that
brought us together
to co-create a life
that will flourish
like wild flowers.

--typewritertroubadour
san diego, ca
sept. 2019

hungover boyfriend

//

confined to the couch
        head pounding
            trying to dicipher
                the memories
        of last night's adventure
                too spent
            to peek through the
                blinds
        after a rendezvous with
            beer, whiskey and wine.
    no glass was left behind
            but thirst can
        only be quenched by liquid
                love and light
        by a girl who
                    still sees
            that the glass is half full
            even when you feel like a
            hungover fool.

//

by typewriter troubadour

san diego, ca 2018 dec 30

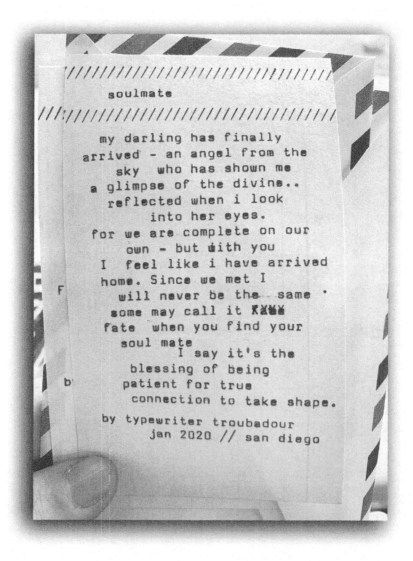

soulmate

my darling has finally
arrived - an angel from the
   sky who has shown me
a glimpse of the divine..
reflected when i look
         into her eyes.
for we are complete on our
    own - but with you
  I feel like i have arrived
home. Since we met I
    will never be the same
some may call it fate
fate when you find your
   soul mate
              I say it's the
    blessing of being
    patient for true
      connection to take shape.

by typewriter troubadour
      jan 2020 // san diego

To Wolf, From Bear

How lucky am I to be trapped
        in such a small space
                with one of my favorite humans?
        Ain't nothing wrong with
                lovin' in a trailer
    work seems like a vacation
            and my insides light up
                    when I see your snaggle toothed
                            grin
            when I clock in
        they say food always tastes
                        better when it is
                    prepared with love
        and that is why
            we are the king and queen
                of the food cart scene

        #typewritertroubadour
            pdx, or
                july 25th, 2015

Story Behind The Poem:

This was written as a gift for someone's co-worker... at a food truck... traded for a delicious falafel pita wrap. Just like food, poetry feeds the soul!

Story Behind The Poem:

This poem was written for a
fellow Typewriter Poet!

It was my first time typing in
Philadelphia where I met
friends of Billimarie.

They told me she had been
writing poems for people, and
this was the first time she had
one done for herself.

Even poets deserve to be the
muse every once in a while.

BILLIMARIE

she shows up
        to the moment
        surrendering to
            the uncertainty
    in an ever expanding
universe,   savor
the sensations of feeling
        grounded in your body
wherever you end up , finding
fascination in the fever
        burning, the branch
breaking, or the siren's
warning that you only have
life to burn, so let
it blaze

BY TYPEWRITER TROUBADOUR
    PHILLY, 2017

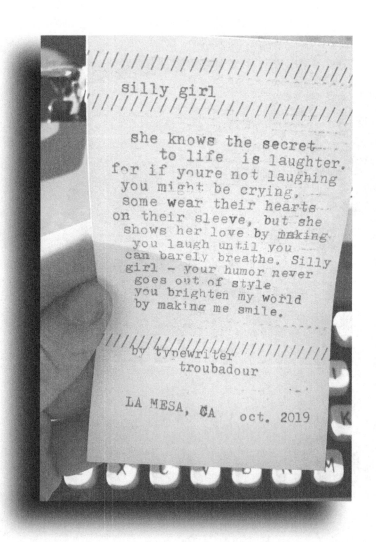

silly girl

she knows the secret
to life is laughter.
for if youre not laughing
you might be crying.
some wear their hearts
on their sleeve, but she
shows her love by making
you laugh until you
can barely breathe. Silly
girl - your humor never
goes out of style
you brighten my world
by making me smile.

by typewriter
troubadour

LA MESA, CA   oct. 2019

the mo on didn't shine
        until I looked
              into yo ur eyes
        and knew that I
              would love you
        until the very
              last star
        burns out of the sky

        typewritertroubadour
              san antonio, tx
                    2017

Bridge

a poem by Jeremy
aka Typewriter
Troubadour

She livens the night,
with a clavé & a chime,
dancing under a full moon
her spirit is free & divine.
She is the magic type,
one who doesn't have to drink
to have a good time,
a gypsy dressed to the nines.
filling strangers souls
with delight, inviting them
into the present moment,
crossing over the bridge,
stepping into a state of bliss.

▽ ▽ ▽ ♥ ▽ ▽ ▽

Story Behind The Poem:

I was in Prescott, Arizona one night on Whiskey Row where I saw a couple of street musicians play. An enchanting woman had wandered over to start a dance party on the sidewalk. A small crowd formed as she passed out egg shakers to strangers. Soon we were all shakin', rattlin', and rollin' underneath the moonlight, having a blast.

People should stop to dance in the streets more often. Everyone wondered what the hell the woman was on — whatever it was — they wanted some of it. Turns out she was sober, and high on life.

At the time, I didn't have my typewriter on me but I was inspired to write her a poem to honor her essence, all the same.

```
*********************************
GINA

*********************************

    He has met his match
      on the tennis court,
        and in his heart
    for Gina keeps him
  on his toes and lifts
  his spirits to the stars.

such magic is like when
  venus connects with mars.
for it's not every day
    you find an ace of
    a girl so beautiful
  it makes your head spin,
  where falling in love
    is a game where both
        people are destined
          to   win.
*********************************
BY TYPEWRITER TROUBADOUR
SAN DIEGO, CA
Commissioned by Zach
```

```
**************************************************
        RAFAEL
**************************************************

        I have fallen under your spell
                Mr. Rafael
        for you fill my heart
                with wonder
            how we share stories
                    across the ocean
                            blue,
                I hope someday
        I can swim out to reach you.
            For the stars you
                put in my eyes
        prove  the future
                is bright,

            I cherish you with
                    all my might
        and no matter
                if its day or night
        I can't get you
                out of my mind,
        you fill my soul
                    with delight.
```

```
*******************************
    Her name is Jessica
 but she may as well be
 called an angel. for her
  sweet grace puts a smile
 on my face and hope in my
 heart. she gave me her love
  right from the start -
   she has never looked at
 me with a judging eye and
  reflects the unconditional
  love of the divine. she
  shared her light as a
   guide that would lead
  me out of the shadows
   and inspired me to show
 up as the best man I can
  be, filling my soul with
  peace and my future with
    possibilities.
*******************************
 by typewriter
    troubadour
   san diego, ca
     sept. 2019
```

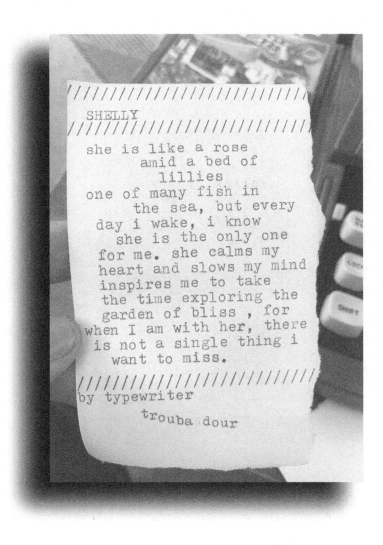

SHELLY

she is like a rose
        amid a bed of
        lillies
one of many fish in
        the sea, but every
day i wake, i know
        she is the only one
for me. she calms my
heart and slows my mind
inspires me to take
the time exploring the
garden of bliss , for
when I am with her, there
is not a single thing i
want to miss.

by typewriter
            trouba dour

23

love and mathematics

///

    our love started as a curiosity
an EQuation that tested my
    IQ . i made a formula
    to solve the mystery
    of your heart. By the
time I got your digits
    I knew my ca lculations
    were correct - that It
        Would take an infinite
            collection of abacuses
    to count the ways
            I adore you.

///

by typewriter troubadour

            san diego, CA

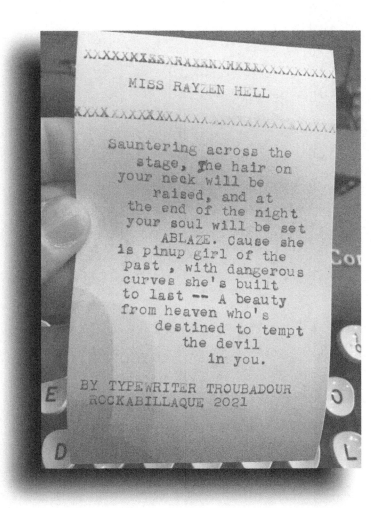

XXXXXXXXSXRAXXXXXXXXXXXXXXXXXX

MISS RAYZEN HELL

XXXXXXXXXXXXXXXXXXXXXXXXXXXXXX

Sauntering across the
    stage, The hair on
your neck will be
    raised, and at
the end of the night
your soul will be set
    ABLAZE. Cause she
is pinup girl of the
past , with dangerous
curves she's built
to last -- A beauty
from heaven who's
    destined to tempt
        the devil
            in you.

BY TYPEWRITER TROUBADOUR
ROCKABILLAQUE 2021

I didn't know the meaning
                 of love
           until I met you
           now my life
                 has new definition
                      and my heart
                           is speechless
           overcome by gratitude
                 for each day
                      I get to spend
                           with you

     by jeremy m brownlowe
          Typewriter Troubadour

L I Z

Loyal and loving,
          sweet as a sap
                    from a tree
           Liz is the perfect
                    lesbian
                         for me.
Soft hearted and kind,
          a handsome face
                    strong and defined,
     What a blessing
               it is
               that this babe
                    is all mine.

BY TYPEWRITER TROUBADOUR

OB, OA   9/2021

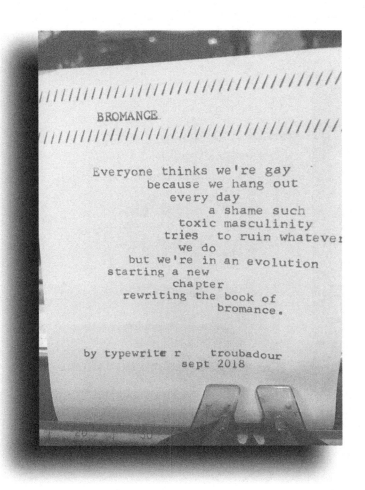

//////////////////////////////////////

BROMANCE

//////////////////////////////////////

Everyone thinks we're gay
        because we hang out
            every day
                a shame such
            toxic masculinity
            tries   to ruin whatever
                we do
        but we're in an evolution
    starting a new
                chapter
            rewriting the book of
                    bromance.

by typewrite r   troubadour
            sept 2018

KOALA BEAR

Wrap your arms around me

    and give me a furry nuzzle

        I love to feel the

    weight of you

        press against me

    as I cradle you

      like

    an endangered   species

by jeremy m brownlowe
    typewriter troubadour
    may 2016
      pdx, or

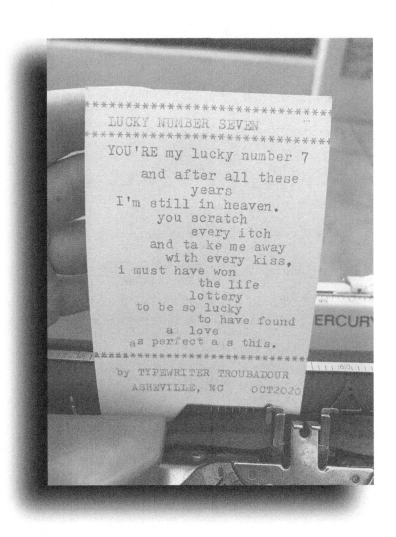

```
*********************************
LUCKY NUMBER SEVEN
*********************************
YOU'RE my lucky number 7
      and after all these
            years
   I'm still in heaven.
      you scratch
            every itch
      and ta ke me away
         with every kiss,
   i must have won
            the life
            lottery
      to be so lucky
            to have found
         a  love
      as perfect a s this.
*********************************
   by TYPEWRITER TROUBADOUR
      ASHEVILLE, NC    OCT2020
```

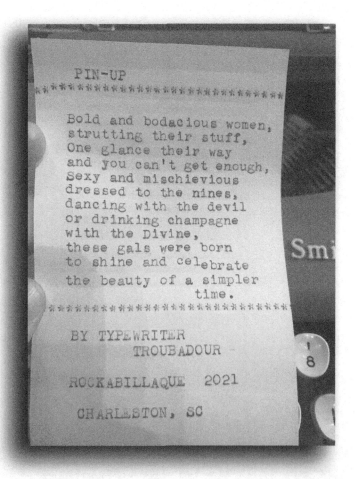

PIN-UP
****

Bold and bodacious women,
strutting their stuff,
One glance their way
and you can't get enough,
Sexy and mischievious
dressed to the nines,
dancing with the devil
or drinking champagne
with the Divine,
these gals were born
to shine and celebrate
the beauty of a simpler
            time.
****

BY TYPEWRITER
        TROUBADOUR

ROCKABILLAQUE 2021

CHARLESTON, SC

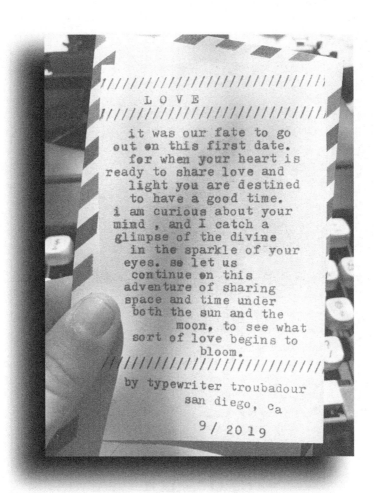

LOVE

it was our fate to go
out on this first date.
for when your heart is
ready to share love and
light you are destined
to have a good time.
i am curious about your
mind , and I catch a
glimpse of the divine
in the sparkle of your
eyes. so let us
continue on this
adventure of sharing
space and time under
both the sun and the
moon, to see what
sort of love begins to
bloom.

by typewriter troubadour
san diego, ca

9/2019

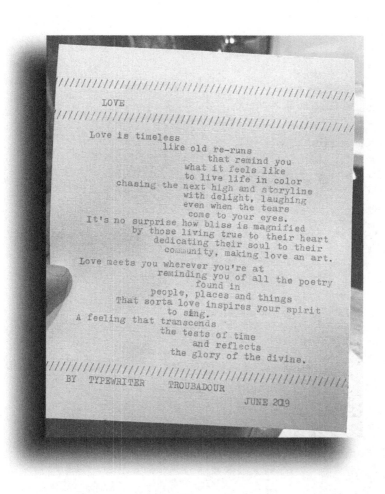

LOVE

Love is timeless
            like old re-runs
                    that remind you
            what it feels like
            to live life in color
    chasing the next high and storyline
            with delight, laughing
            even when the tears
            come to your eyes.
    It's no surprise how bliss is magnified
        by those living true to their heart
            dedicating their soul to their
            community, making love an art.

Love meets you wherever you're at
        reminding you of all the poetry
                found in
            people, places and things
        That sorta love inspires your spirit
            to sing.
    A feeling that transcends
                the tests of time
                    and reflects
                the glory of the divine.

BY TYPEWRITER   TROUBADOUR

                                JUNE 2019

Pro Tip:
Buying someone a poem on
your first date will
probably get you a second
one.

PART TWO:

Passion

Eros induced passion, new crushes
and infatuation, poems that will
make your heart pulse.

Poets are known for getting a little carried away. You probably know that feeling. That fresh feeling of falling in love. The feeling when you meet someone new and are totally intrigued by their magic it's hard to think about anything else.

Maybe you're the type who's easily inspired by the suspense in getting to know someone new. Or perhaps you have found your mate, and find new ways to fall in love. Love can be dangerous. Love can lift your heart like a hot air balloon. If love is about taking a risk, there is probably a poem about it.

Whoever you are, if you like a juicy love story, these poems are for you.

If you feel inspired read these aloud to the one you adore.

```
        500 miles
////////////////////////////////////
      i drove south, 500 miles
    lured by mystery
      this girl intrigues me
      for she is already
        a wild ride
        she brings stars
        to my eyes
                on this
      adventure
          she has taken
      the wheel
      xx      already
              beginning
        to drive me a little
        insane.

////////////////////////////////////

      by typewriter troubadour
            san diego, ca
```

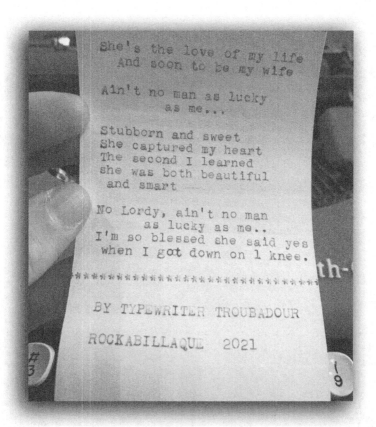

She's the love of my life
   And soon to be my wife

Ain't no man as lucky
         as me...

Stubborn and sweet
She captured my heart
The second I learned
she was both beautiful
and smart

No Lordy, ain't no man
         as lucky as me..
I'm so blessed she said yes
when I got down on 1 knee.

****

BY TYPEWRITER TROUBADOUR

ROCKABILLAQUE   2021

//

ADVENTURE

// ////

you send a thrill
down my spin
whenever I look
into your eyes
for we are on the
Journey of a lifetime
where we are headed
straight to
the center of
each other's soul

//

BY TYPEWRITER TROUBADOUR
PDX, 2017

```
*************************************************

    L O V E    &    R O A D   T R I P S

*************************************************

        Each day is a new adventure
           whether we are on a road
                  trip
          showing each other all
             of the sacred sights,
          weaving our stories
                  together
           like lovers on the run
           falling deeper in love
        at     each mile marker
                 as we spread
            our love all over
                  the map.


*************************************************


    BY TYPEWRITER TROUBADOUR
    CARPINTERIA, CA
    SEPT. 2021
    FOR KAYLA & LOGAN
```

sometimes life is like a movie
or a miracle -
that fated moment when you
land a seat next to a
soul you were destined
to meet. who knew
this is where our story
would take off - xxxx on an
adventure as close to heaven
as a plane can fly, sharing
an armrest with an angel
was a total delight - a love
that keeps my head in the clouds
now, years later my feet still
won't touch the ground knowing
I found the one who makes me
feel like I'm on top
of the world.

by typewriter troubadour
palm springs, ca
march 2019

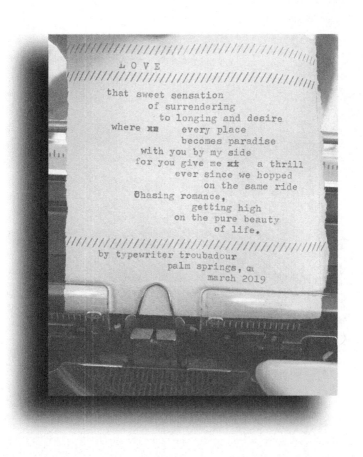

L O V E

that sweet sensation
        of surrendering
            to longing and desire
where xm   every place
            becomes paradise
    with you by my side
    for you give me xk   a thrill
            ever since we hopped
                on the same ride
    Chasing romance,
                getting high
        on the pure beauty
                of life.

by typewriter troubadour
        palm springs, ca
                march 2019

It's Friday night
         and I don't ever want the dawn to come
               I want to do   all
                        the positions
            with you
                     my sweet dear
         for while we are animals
         I want to feel the kiss
            of the heavens
   keep my eyes open
                        to breathe
            into your tantric
                        soul fuck
         holler out in tongues
                  rejoicing
                           in the spirit
         of the flesh
                  molding into
                        a smolder
                  we can bring back to
                           life

   by jeremy M. Brownlowe
            aug 7th, 2015
               pdx, or

                     #typewritertroubadour

41

XXXXXX   MY BELOVED XXXXXX

          My heart beats red
            for you my dear
              truly read me
        oh how I have waited
            so many lonely cold nights
                  the typical yearning
          of a soul unfed
            xwxixingxix   and then you
          walked in
                  with your perfect reckless
                        nature
            I would learn to tame
              make you come crawling
              willingly
            into my bed
        so these fierce
                  winter nights
              would melt away
                      the coldness
        we have weathered in the outside world

          by jeremy m brownlowe
                      #typewritertroubadour
              pdx, or
                  oct 16. 2015

42

When the ocean met the sky...
water and air
kissed
and came together
the orign
of creation
so wet
and
heavy under
the earth's pull
the birth of the horizon

by jeremy m brownlowe
typewriter troubadour
pdx, or
june 2016

////////////////////////////////////

L O V E

////////////////////////////////////

new love fills your heart
where you look at a person
as if they are a work of art
you could gaze at them
forever like they are a
lucky star
thathas shot thru the dark
to bring light back
into your world.
////////////////////////////////////

by typewriter
troubadour
santa monica, ca 2016

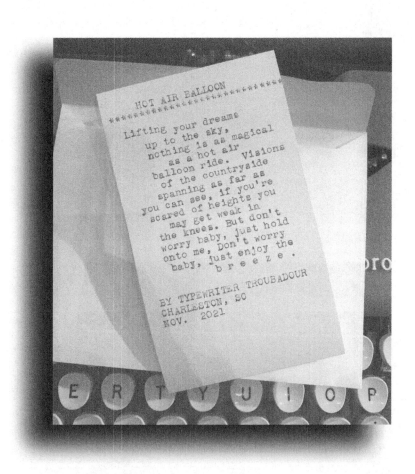

HOT AIR BALLOON

Lifting your dreams
up to the sky,
nothing is as magical
as a hot air
balloon ride. Visions
of the countryside
spanning as far as
you can see, if you're
scared of heights you
may get weak in
the knees. But don't
worry baby, just hold
onto me, Don't worry
baby, just enjoy the
breeze.

BY TYPEWRITER TROUBADOUR
CHARLESTON, SC
NOV. 2021

SEXY EYES

I am so turned on by your sexy eyes

                I want to swim naked in them

                    taste the salt

            as it leaks down your cheek

                You entrance me

                with your gaze

        I want to spend the rest of my days

                        searching

                        for

                    your soul

    a poem by jeremy m brownlowe

            typewriter troubadour

LOVE

Love written in red
        and screamed for balconies
                just for you
        the complex kind
        that makes a poet go mad
            ax   the sweet kind
            that makes men
            weak in the knees
        overcome by the strength
                found in the beloved's arms
        so many types of love
                some that threatens to kill
                some that
                    promises to heal
        no matter the kind
                it always manages
            to make us
                    feel alive
            and will always be there
        for better
                    or for worse

        by jeremy m brownlowe
            typewriter troubadour
                    BEND, OR
            spring 2016

46

Salvador
How you entrance me
Your face a mirror
Your body a statue
Your love like armor
Strong and protective
At first glance
feelings were abstract
Foreign from words
Now I see clear and vibrant
Colors inspired by sunsets
You have awakened me
as dawn summons
the first glint of morning.

PANDEMIC LOVE
****
i want to take off
    your mask
and the rest of your
    clothes
because you're the
one I want to be with
    in this weird, weird
    world.. Love is a
virus I caught the
second I saw you
        and
    quarantining
    during our honeymoon
is my dream
    come true.

****
FOR KATIE & PETER
BY TYPEWRITERTROUBADOUR
ASHEVILLE, NC
        OCT 2020

```
          LOVE
that moment when your heart
              pumps the deepest shade of red
                and you feel the blood
                pound in your temple
              waiting to see your new crush
                beyond your daydreams
              where the time always ticks a little
                too slow
          until you are together in real time
                a place where life has never felt
                so vivid
              and each inch closer seems like
          you are looking over a cliff
                and are finally brave to say 'fuck it'
                and dive off to see what sort of bliss
                will catch you in a kiss


      by jeremy m brownlowe

                        typewritertroubadour
          pdx, or      aug 2016
```

//

You get stuck in my head
        like a song
        that spea ks
            directly to my soul.
For i have been sea rching
    for you like a rare record ,
        sifting through
        bins of shit
    to finally find the person
        you knew in **my**
        heart was it.
Now I wear my heart on my
        sleeve , **kno**wing it isnt
    as gruesome as it seems when
    you love a person who is
        both a punk and grounded
        like a rock.

by typewriter troubadour
        la mesa, ca
                    june 2019

//

XXX

Love and Romance the killer, the thriller, the heart beat
                that keeps us dancing in the fire despite
                the burns we risk for the flame

XXXXXXXXXXXXXXXXXXXXXXXXXXXXXXXXXXXXXXXXXXXXXXXXXXXXXXXXXXX

                    by jeremy m brownlowe
                        typewriter troubadour
                            pdx, or
                            june 2016

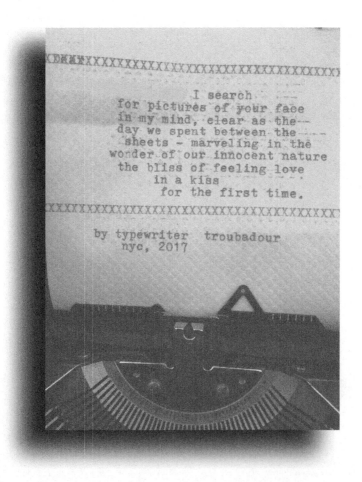

XXXXXXXXXXXXXXXXXXXXXXXXXXXXXXXXXXXXXXXXX

```
            I search
   for pictures of your face
   in my mind, clear as the
   day we spent between the
     sheets - marveling in the
   wonder of our innocent nature
   the bliss of feeling love
        in a kiss
          for the first time.
```

XXXXXXXXXXXXXXXXXXXXXXXXXXXXXXXXXXXXXXXXX

```
   by typewriter  troubadour
      nyc, 2017
```

52

```
********************************
my lady
      my mistress
   how I wish to tame you
 for you are wild
    and feral
       like a cat in the night
     i crave the sensations
    of your claw
        scrawling red upon
  my skin
          oh  how i wish to
        devour the sin you
         demand from my
  innermost longing
            as you welcome
              me to your
               lips
          i cannot resist

********************************
 a poem written by jeremy
         typewritertroubadour
     pdx, or      nov 2016
```

```
*********************************************************
      P L E A S U R E
*********************************************************


That dizzy perfection

            so elated i forgot I had
                  eyes
                  a nose
                  a mouth
                  and fingers

            because I become my senses
                  one by one

      no longer apart from my
                  surroundings

      and there is no future
                  or a pull from past recollections

      when you feel such pleasure
                  to the point where you
                        forget your name
            the rest of the world won't

                  feel quite  the  same
```

CRUSH

that moment when you can feel a tingle
a spark of electric magic before your
fingers even brush skin in curious
affection, the air stills,despite the
wind pushing you forward and back.you
can almost see each other's breath. that
xixnxxxix craving to know, to hold,to
explore new territories of another's most
intimate landscape. but only certain
seasons bear fruit, and so you drink to
ease off the frost and the fear of being
frozen in isolation. for we are pack
animals just hungry for a little bit of
loyalty and love. can you give me a piece
of your heart, a taste of your mouth, a
steadfast certainty , because I am all up
in my head thinking about what you would
be like if you were to join me in bed

          BY TYPEWRITER TROUBADOUR
              LAFAYETTE , LA 2017

PRIESTESS OF PLEASURE   II

****

savoring every sensation
of the sacred feminine
the priestess of pleasure
pursues the pulse of having
her buttons pushed just
right. she puts her passion
into action , always on
a mission to share her
satisfaction . Bor she
knows the secret to life
can be shared with both
a spank and a kiss and
each moment of connection
was designed to give you
a taste of eternal bliss.

****

BY TYPEWRITER
       TROUBADOUR

BOR CELIA LOVELOVELOVE

****

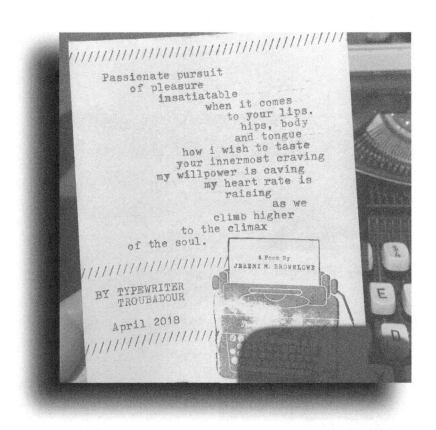

Passionate pursuit
of pleasure
insatiatable
when it comes
to your lips,
hips, body
and tongue
how i wish to taste
your innermost craving
my willpower is caving
my heart rate is
raising
as we
climb higher
to the climax
of the soul.

A Poem By
JEREMY M. BROWNLOWE

BY TYPEWRITER
TROUBADOUR

April 2018

Story Behind The Poem:

Why, Yes. Sometimes reading
these poems aloud to other
people's lovers in public
places is a little... awkward.

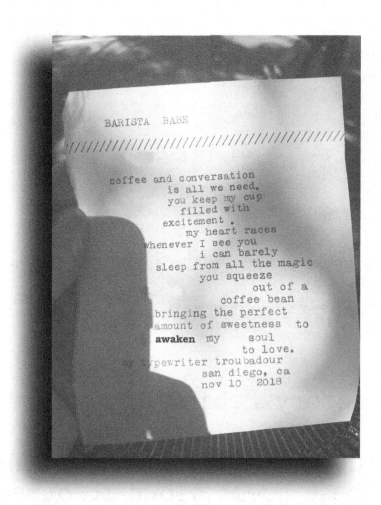

BARISTA BABE
///

coffee and conversation
        is all we need.
      you keep my cup
        filled with
      excitement .
          my heart races
whenever I see you
          i can barely
      sleep from all the magic
          you squeeze
                out of a
              coffee bean
    bringing the perfect
  amount of sweetness to
awaken my   soul
          to love.
  by typewriter troubadour
        san diego, ca
        nov 10 2018

58

as a photographer
                i have a trained eye
                    and you
                              have caught mine
            while I looked
                    for the details
                        in a man I was destined
                                    to love
            I found kindness
                        in your heart
                            comfort in your arms
                        and loyalty
                                    in your gaze
            and now we continue
                    to chase
                and capture
                        both the beauty
                            and simple
                                    moments
                            we   share
                                together
                        now that we know
                the bigge r picture
                    of what it means
                            to love some one
                            and be fully seen

        a poem by typewritertroubadour
                            de c. 2016

love is a mix tape

each man has taught me a different song
one taught me how the soul cries out
to release the spirit
of the blues
another opened my mind

with the swirling sounds
of psychedelic rock
reverberating
my soul
until I couldn't
tell bravado from vibrato
another taught me the rhythm of voice
and the messages of xxxixi
justice and high rollers
hip to the beat

now i am no longer with these men
no longer a blank sheet
for notes to be
dropped

and while love for these men has left
my heart

the love of music is the soundtrack of
our   romance   still burns strong

by jeremy m brownlowe
typewritertroubadour

pdx, or   aug 2016

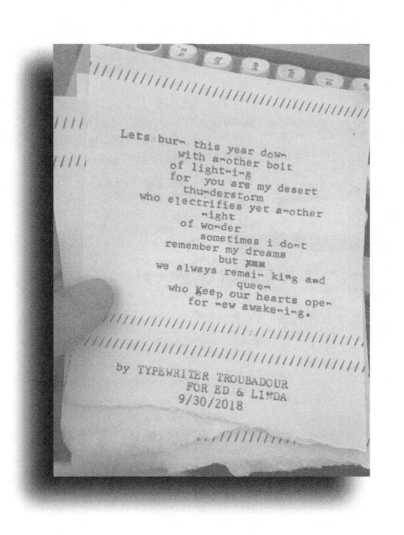

Lets burn this year down
    with another bolt
of lighting
for you are my desert
    thunderstorm
who electrifies yet another
    night
of wonder
    sometimes i dont
remember my dreams
    but xxm
we always remain king and
    queen
who keep our hearts open
    for new awakening.

by TYPEWRITER TROUBADOUR
    FOR ED & LINDA
    9/30/2018

```
***************************************
    Darin, Darren, I don't even
know how to spell your name,
but yet I want to study you, you
   -- your body
   -- your mind
   -- your soul
        even for just one night
and I am sorry if i caused
     a fright
but I am really just a guy
    looking to share a little
    space and time
and I couldn't leave town
     without sending you
   the message that I
   wish you would be mine
***************************************

   by typewritertroubadour
   new orleans, 2017

   commissioned by Terence
```

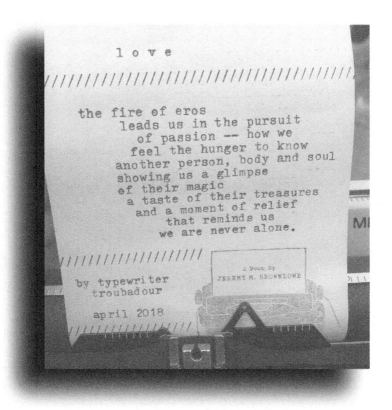

love

///

the fire of eros
        leads us in the pursuit
            of passion -- how we
        feel the hunger to know
    another person, body and soul
    showing us a glimpse
    of their magic
        a taste of their treasures
        and a moment of relief
            that reminds us
            we are never alone.

////////////////////

by typewriter
   troubadour

april 2018

A Poem By
JEREMY M. BROWNLOWE

PART THREE: Devotion

Love Conquers All.

Love ain't always easy.

Sometimes we may find we are not on the same page as our partners. It may be difficult finding the right words to say, and you may find yourself hiring a poet to help you out.

Truth is, sometimes even the people we love the most can annoy the hell out of us.

Relationships take work, and trying to balance work, school, kids, or life's demands can put pressure on a relationship.

Sometimes sacrifices need to be made, and partners must separate for a spell. But what doesn't ultimately end the connection, makes it stronger... so they say.

Love ain't always easy, but if it's meant to be... it's worth it.

BALL AND CHAIN

we have the power to reclaim
    the term ball and chain ..
cause if there was ever someone
to share a cell in the prison of
love I would pray to the heavens above
that I would be serving time with you.
    You have my heart on lockdown and
I am happy to throw away the key
for you are the perfect person for
me. if loving someone so much was a
crime, i'd plead guilty and gladly
serve time. for love likes ours
    is the only thing that has
        ever really made me feel
the   freedom   to   step into

        authenticity.

```
we weren't built
      for  fair weather
we   were built for  heavy
        snow and storm  -
love as   the     compass
        that gives direction
        through the detours
              navigating
                    the ebb
        and flow of human
              nature  proving
                    our love
        was built to last
```

by typewriter troubadour
    santa monica, ca 2017.

```
XXXXIXXXXXXXXIXXXXXXXIXXXXXXIXXXXXXIXXXXIXXXXXXIXXXXXIXXXXX
```

you are as rare
                as a raindrop
                        in the desert
        who has filled me with abundance
        my glass overflowing
                with mutual understanding
I have craved you
                like the soil craves the rain
                        after a drought
        oh how I wish to be in your arms
                saturated with your scent
                as if I had been
                dancing in the showers
                        of a summer storm
                two hearts, two minds
                        waiting so long
                                to combine
        now entranced by wild intrigue
                that I hope will
                        continue to bloom

A Poem By Typewriter Troubadour

2016

```
XXXXXXXXXIXXXXXXIXXXXXXXIXXXXXXIXXXXXXPXXXIXXXXPXXXIXXXXPXXIXXX
```

                PETRICHOR

when you look at me
          you break through
        to the other side
      where all my secrets
                  hopes and dreams
              live
      if I am brave I can share
              myself
          my true authentic self
          my soul
      and when the fear disappears
          and I see you waiting past
              the gates
      I can see you fully also

                              may 2, 2015
                              brooklyn, NY

70

FOR   ADRIENNE & GENE

a poem by TYPEWRITERTROUBADOUR
. . . .

it has been a wild
          ride
     some bumps
          along the way
but love is a journey
     sometimes
     exploring off course
          to get back on
          track
and feel the thrill
of sharing a life
     with someone
commited to love
     beyond beauty
     beyond the ugly
     just because you can't
imagine doing it any different

///
    25 YEARS
///

        We have shared many seasons ,
              celebrations
                    and sorrow
        a nd still we stick it out
              to do it again
                    tomorrow .
        for when i met you
              it was the moment
                    i knew
        i found love that was
              pure and true.
        I wouldnt take back any
              day or any night
        if it would keep you by
        my side for another
        25 years of life
              and countin' on.
///
        by typewriter
              troubadour

              portland, or
                    august 2019

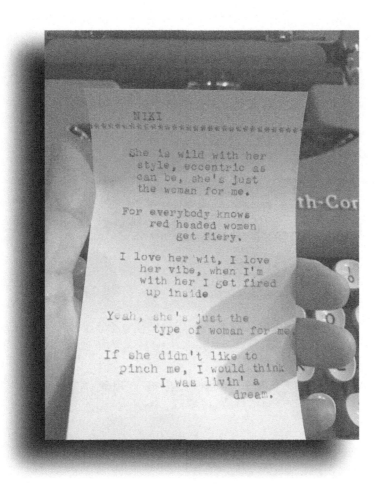

NIKI

She is wild with her
style, eccentric as
can be, she's just
the woman for me.

For everybody knows
red headed women
get fiery.

I love her wit, I love
her vibe, when I'm
with her I get fired
up inside

Yeah, she's just the
type of woman for me.

If she didn't like to
pinch me, I would think
I was livin' a
dream.

```
------------------------------------------------
love love
------------------------------------------------


fa ll    in love with love
              sometimes it is a bed
              full of bliss
          sometimes it teaches
              forgiveness
but love keeps us connected
          like glue ,
          history I couldnt think
          of sharing with anyone
              but you..

      for you have shown up
          time and time again
          proving love is a story
              that will
                  never end.


      by TYPEWRITER TROUBADOUR
              SAVANNAH, GA
                  NOV. 2020
```

CHRISTA

****

you have seen me
in my darkest hour ,
an angel who reminds me
of my power. Love whose
mission is to have no
condition – and carves
out a space where I
can feel safe to
make friends with my
demons. With no demand
you are there to try and
understand the
complexity of
being human, and
with you by my side
I remember that
true love serves as
a light that will
guide me back to a
place of peace.

** TYPEWRITER
TROUBADOUR

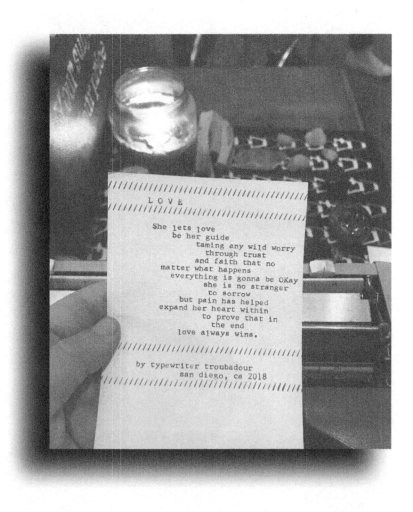

LOVE

She lets love
be her guide
taming any wild worry
through trust
and faith that no
matter what happens
everything is gonna be OKay
she is no stranger
to sorrow
but pain has helped
expand her heart within
to prove that in
the end
love always wins.

by typewriter troubadour
san diego, ca 2018

RELATIONSHIP

****

We show up
        even though it scares us
        to show our true colors
        can be messy
    and leave a mark.
but there is always a place
    for XXX   love in my heart
        and love takes
    patience, strength and
    forgiving our authenticities
        that may have the
        best intentions but
        still rub us the wrong
    way, knowing that each day
        at the end, love always
        wins, if we let it.

****

        by TYPEWRITER TROUBADOUR

```
****************************************

          FAMILY
****************************************

When push comes to shove
            we show up
                full  force
            armed with love.
For we stick together
                through thick
                    and thin,
            always carrying
            the spirit
            of  family within.
We know how to turn a
            frown into a grin,
cause when the world
            gets tough,
we know  family
            is the best medicine.


        by typewriter troubadour
            cant.on,  GA

****************************************
```

///////////////////////////////////

we speak in different
tongues, wrapping them
around a new language
of love. for I don't have
to use words to feel your
heart melt in my hand --
can my tender touch help
you understand the poetry
I cannot deliver upon the
page ? can you feel my
desire as I gently stroke
your face? your words
ma y not fit in my mouth
but my kiss lands
on your lips
and transcends
any translation
of bliss.

///////////////////////////////////

by typewriter troubadour
san diego, ca
sept. 2019

"language barriers & love"

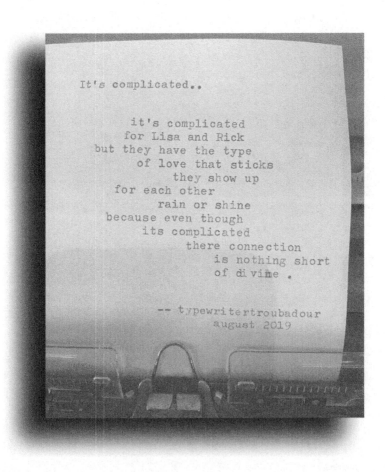

It's complicated..

it's complicated
for Lisa and Rick
but they have the type
of love that sticks
they show up
for each other
rain or shine
because even though
its complicated
there connection
is nothing short
of divine .

-- typewritertroubadour
august 2019

```
partnership
*****************************************
    no matter the storm
            that blows in our path
             threatening to wreck
                 and shake our
        foundations
    we will stand strong
            and remain faithful
        to our roots
             for this is how
        true love blooms
                allowing each other
                to grow
             vowing not to break
                when a cold wind
                blows


*****************************************
    by jeremy m brownlowe
            typewriter troubadour
                nov 2016
```

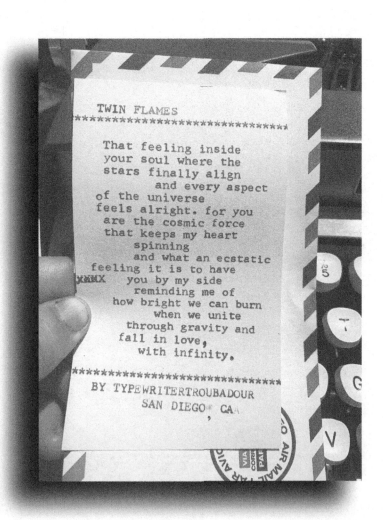

TWIN FLAMES
****

That feeling inside
your soul where the
stars finally align
        and every aspect
of the universe
feels alright. for you
are the cosmic force
that keeps my heart
        spinning
        and what an ecstatic
feeling it is to have
xXMX   you by my side
        reminding me of
how bright we can burn
        when we unite
        through gravity and
fall in love,
        with infinity.

****

BY TYPEWRITERTROUBADOUR
        SAN DIEGO, CA

there is laundry
    to be washed   ,
        dishes to be done
    and   which proves we have
    that dirty kind of love
one that is so full of passion
   its hard to take action
for it's easier to pick up
    a poem than it is to pick up
   a broom, still -- you are
the only one I
want in the
bedroom - even
though it is
   constantly
   a mess , I am
glad we found each
other in the our
   quest of love.

TYPEWRITER
   TROUBADOUR

A Poem By
JEREMY M. BROWNLOWE

```
/////////////////////////////////////////
LONG DISTANCE LOVE
/////////////////////////////////////////
Lover  -  feel my longing
   cross the country, the desert
       and the sea . I count
    ea ch   da y    down on
    the calendar  until the day
you come ba ck  to me. Lover
     you ha ve  done a number
              on  me.
Each  night  your a  drea m
       shimmering upon every
              star
Lover, I've been yours from
        the very start.
I'd travel the world just to
      give you my hea rt.
Lover, time could never tear
        our souls a part.

/////////////////////////////////////////
by typewriter troubadour
          DA MESA, CA
     may 3? 2019
```

```
/////////////////////////////////////////////
     this is the    part
                  where we
                embrace the
              shadows
     and trudge ahead with bravery
              for our love has a
                  purpose
              a test that will make
     us stronger in the end. for no
     valley is too deep, no
              unknown exploration
                too daunting
       when we carry the torch
              of our love
       letting hope be our guide.
/////////////////////////////////////////////
       by typewriter troubadour
                san diego, ca
                  sept 16, 2018
```

```
///////////////////////////////////
DC
///////////////////////////////////
```

Just when I thought
   I reached my edge

I see your face in
   the horizon.
A curious wonder
   and endless possibility
where I feel my body,
   heart, spirit , and
   soul unite in the
healing flow of love.
Where my past is washed
clean and smooth like a
stone I thought hopeless
worry had hardened. But
  you have seen me in my
entireity across continents
of joys we have yet to
explore, and a universe of
bliss that washes away all

worries with the thought of

    Your kiss.

//
difficulties in communicating
//
deciphering the meaning of the feelings
That whirl inside my body and mind
struggling to find the words that
fit , without a dictionary in sight.
sentences are jumbled the moment they
pour from my lips into the light.
can you hear what I am desperately
trying to say by silently looking
into my eyes? can you see what
lies underneath the mask of confusion
and pride? I long to show you my
truth and share my story and leave
my heart and ears to take in yours
so we can be on the same page
or at least become a phrase
embedded in the same book.
//

by typewriter troubadour
san diego, ca 2019 april 28
//

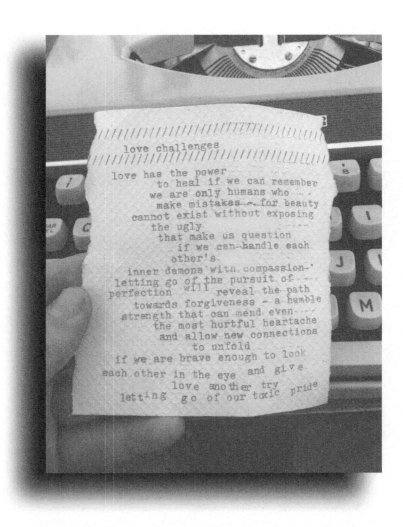

love challenges

love has the power
        to heal if we can remember
    we are only humans who
        make mistakes—for beauty
cannot exist without exposing
    the ugly
        that make us question
            if we can handle each
            other's
    inner demons with compassion
letting go of the pursuit of
perfection will reveal the path
    towards forgiveness — a humble
strength that can mend even
        the most hurtful heartache
        and allow new connections
            to unfold
    if we are brave enough to look
each other in the eye and give
            love another try
    letting go of our toxic pride

LINDA

****

i have never stopped
        loving you
    and regret where my heart
        has skipped a beat
    for I wish the pulse
        could be heard
    loud as a drum
for y ou   are a revolution
    one who inspires me
  to be a better man
    whose wisdom is beyond any
        other woman

            and has taught me
    to understand love's power
      to bring about Change

a poem commissioned by Marlon
    written by typewritertroubadour
        tucson, az
            2017

//
    Love & Self Reflection
//

        love inspires us to look
              in the mirror, dive
        deep into our souls,
              and uncover all
        the stories destined to
              be told.   when you
        show up fully to another
        you   can't help but feel
              a little vulnerable
        and exposed. but love is
        a container, a sacred space
        for you to explore secrets
              of your shadow, bringing
        your truth to the light
              that illuminates
              the path to trusting
        you are   enough   , worthy
        of giving and receiving
              an abundance of love
        that will help shape you into
              the greatest version of
                         self.

        by typewritertroubador   sd, ca 2019

//

There will be pa ssion
        for it runs in our blood
    we are the type of people
      who are serious about
          our love. marria ge
  is sacred like the sta rs
        up above. for we are
  legends bound to honor our name.
    we will tell it like it is -
  we'll be loya l   vowing
              to praise
      each other for the rest
        of our da ys. we cannot
    deny we wound up together
  by fate. destined to serve and
  surrender to being team ma tes.
  love can be a ga mble, but with
      you, I'm playing to win.
//

    by typewriter troubadour
          la mesa ,   ca 2019

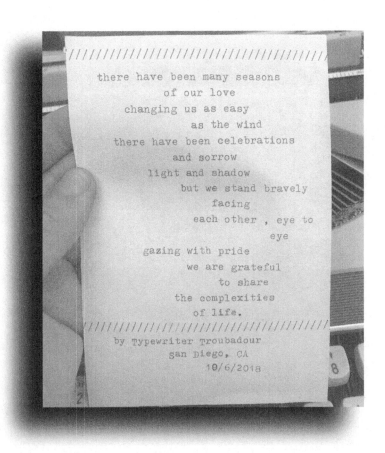

///
there have been many seasons
of our love
changing us as easy
as the wind
there have been celebrations
and sorrow
light and shadow
but we stand bravely
facing
each other , eye to
eye
gazing with pride
we are grateful
to share
the complexities
of life.
///
by Typewriter Troubadour
San Diego, CA
10/6/2018

```
!****************************
  LOVE CONQUERS ALL
 !****************************

  When the cold night
        rolls in
  and the sky begins
        to shake
  with thunder, and you're
     filled with fear like
  no other, come back,
     take cover, because
     love conquers all.
  No mark in the sand too
     deep, no secret so
  strong to keep, when
     love  conquers  us all.
        surrender, surrender..
  because love conquers all.

 !****************************

  by typewriter
        troubadour

     joshua tree  musicfest
           2019
```

PART FOUR:

Lost Love

Some love stories
weren't meant to last forever.

That doesn't mean they aren't
still worthy of a poem.

Sometimes love stories don't last.

It has been said that some people come into our lives for a reason, a season, or a lifetime...

Even if we find a partner to grow with us throughout the years, one person's story will end in tears, as death is destined to knock on even the most devoted partnership's door.

These poems honor the lovers that left our lives for whatever reason, to the ones who are isolated in their loneliness, in hopes of serving as a reminder they are not alone in their pain.

These poems reflect the heartache, the longing, and the teachings our previous partners offered us in their absence so we could learn to love ourselves.

L O V E

the full spectrum
    of bliss
        where love transforms
        you with a single kiss
        but ~~imaginexthe~~
        the heart can howl
        like a beast of the
        lonely wild
feeling alone in a crowd
    when the only person
    you want to have
    around is nowhere to
        be found.

by typewritertroubadour
    ~~Ypxxjxax~~   NYC 2017

TO REMEMBER YOU BY
///
    i'll always remember the
                color of your eyes
    the way the sunlight shined upon
            your face
        how tender you made my heart
                feel
    butterflys remind me of you
            for all the joy they
                bring to each summer
                    flower
    if this love was only meant to
        last a season, I will
        always remember you
            the moment the rain
    brings new   color to
            the fields in spring.
///
        by typewriter troubadour
            san diego, ca 2018

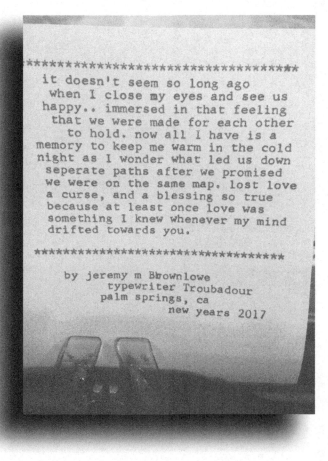

****
it doesn't seem so long ago
  when I close my eyes and see us
happy.. immersed in that feeling
  that we were made for each other
    to hold. now all I have is a
memory to keep me warm in the cold
night as I wonder what led us down
  seperate paths after we promised
  we were on the same map. lost love
  a curse, and a blessing so true
  because at least once love was
  something I knew whenever my mind
  drifted towards you.

****

    by jeremy m Brownlowe
        typewriter Troubadour
      palm springs, ca
              new years 2017

A month has passed

  and I can't get you out

    of my mind

my tongue is tied

    over all the stories I could

  tell you to inspire you like I once did

      for I miss you

          and feel myself unraveling

      each day we are apart

  I miss your room and how you have

      a taste for chaos

  how you would show off

          standing on your head

  and now my world is turned upside down

      in your absense

wondering why everything is so complicated

  when I treasure simple moments

      like watching you

        open pistachios

          cracked open

  like my heart

            the day you released me
            back into the wild

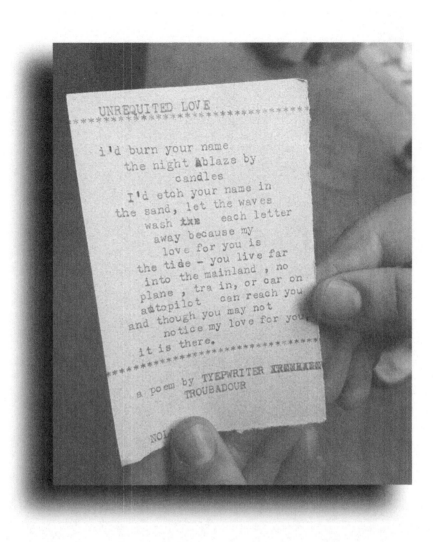

UNREQUITED LOVE
****

i'd burn your name
    the night Ablaze by
        candles
    I'd etch your name in
the sand, let the waves
    wash the   each letter
    away because my
        love for you is
the tide - you live far
    into the mainland , no
    plane , tra in, or car on
    autopilot   can reach you
and though you may not
    notice my love for you,
    it is there.
****

a poem by TYEPWRITER XXXXXXX
        TROUBADOUR

    NOL

100

```
              LUST      VS      LOVE


lust is the vice that drives
              us crazy
                        twisting and turning
                          over the muse
                feeling so used
                yet hoping to be tamed
        lust   makes us sweat
                      even when we are
                                  left in the cold
        meanwhile
                love
                      plays no games
                love sees each of us
                      as equal
              it wants to fill our souls
                        until we overflow
                  totally satisfied
                            feeling at home
                able to survive
                      without
        the      drama   of    heartache




              by jeremy m brownlowe
                          typewriter troubadour
                    pdx, or
                            spring 2016
```

TINY MIRRORS

When I stare into your eyes

        I see a series of tiny mirrors

      sometimes it is a funhouse

        sometimes it is a horror show

as I allow you to get to know me

      and I you

     it takes bravery

      to see the truth
          staring back

   no airbrush
         no cover up

     but it's real, something

i would never
shatter

by jeremy m brownlowe
      Typewriter Troubadour
      pdx, or
        may 2016

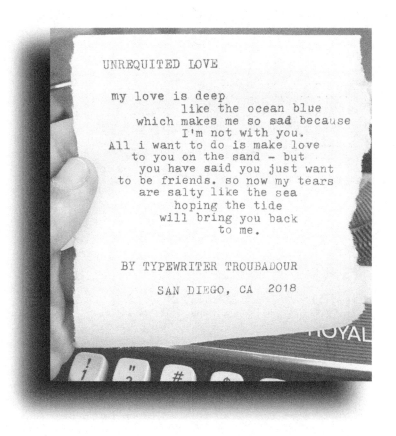

UNREQUITED LOVE

my love is deep
            like the ocean blue
      which makes me so sad because
         I'm not with you.
All i want to do is make love
   to you on the sand – but
      you have said you just want
   to be friends. so now my tears
      are salty like the sea
         hoping the tide
         will bring you back
               to me.

BY TYPEWRITER TROUBADOUR

      SAN DIEGO, CA   2018

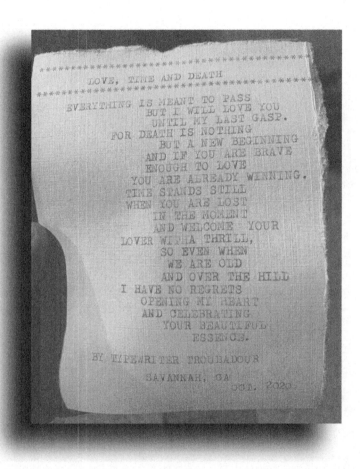

LOVE, TIME AND DEATH

EVERYTHING IS MEANT TO PASS
BUT I WILL LOVE YOU
UNTIL MY LAST GASP.
FOR DEATH IS NOTHING
BUT A NEW BEGINNING
AND IF YOU ARE BRAVE
ENOUGH TO LOVE
YOU ARE ALREADY WINNING.
TIME STANDS STILL
WHEN YOU ARE LOST
IN THE MOMENT
AND WELCOME YOUR
LOVER WITH A THRILL,
SO EVEN WHEN
WE ARE OLD
AND OVER THE HILL
I HAVE NO REGRETS
OPENING MY HEART
AND CELEBRATING
YOUR BEAUTIFUL
ESSENCE.

BY TYPEWRITER TROUBADOUR

SAVANNAH, GA

OCT. 2020

```
      unrequited love
*******************************

      i would give you
            My heart
              my soul
                my mind
                and my time
      I'd give you my lips
            my hips
            and a sexy look
            from my eye
      but you only give me
            a cold shoulder
            and a wish to
            dream on
      that someday this
        infatuation will
      actually be mutual
*******************************

      BY TYPEWRITER
                TROUBADOUR
```

Story Behind The Poem:

Whenever I'm approached by someone who wants a poem to honor a breakup, I usually ask a couple questions first...

Do they want a poem to reflect their misery and heartache? Or do they want something to put themselves on a positive path for the future?

This person wanted a poem to reflect the mutual love and respect she and her former partner still held for each other.

Sometimes romantic relationships don't work out — but if there is still a connection the relationship can transform into a valuable friendship.

LOVE & DEATH & THE AFTERLIFE

****

eventually even though we vow

to never leave each other's

side, we will have to part ways

even for just a spell, the one

left behind will feel the breath

of hell in every waking moment

without the love of his life. for

now we are each other's definition

of heaven, and if there is any faith

in the unknown we vow to find each

other after xxxh   the final

heart beats

```
/////////////////////////////////////////////
  heartbreak
/////////////////////////////////////////////

  Light leaks through the cracks
          relieving you of
          the darkness
       that lost love awakened
             releasing
                 the tragedy of
          those who ran away
          too soon
             to challenge xxx
  you    to rediscover the
          love we can carry
                for ourselves.

/////////////////////////////////////////////

  by typewriter troubadour
          san diego, ca 2018

/////////////////////////////////////////////
```

Story Behind The Poem:

Wayback in the day, I was typing outside the Portland Night Market. It was winter and freezing outside, a struggle to keep my fingers warm waiting for the next muse to arrive.

Eventually, a woman in her fifties approached me, and said she wanted a poem about her partner who had terminal cancer. Though she had a request. She didn't want me to sugar coat it. She didn't want a poem that suggested her partner was going to recover. She knew her partner would soon pass away, and wanted a poem to reflect this terrible fate. I can't remember if I read the poem to her or if she saved it for later. I just hope that the poem helped her on her journey forward while honoring a love that is infinite.

LOVE AFTER DEATH

****

even though
you have left this world
i still feel you with me
for my heart is now
where you will reside
- always -
no passing of time
can make you fade
away
because i still miss you every day
and i think ofall of the things
we would say and do
whenever i see something
that reminds me of you
it may seem like i
am talking to an imaginary friend
for those who don't understand
that love doesn't go away
when the spirit leaves
the body of your soulmate
and you are left standing
with a love that still grows
without end

by jeremy m brownlowe   typewritertroubadour

pdx, or   aug 2016

Story Behind The Poem

During the final formatting stages of this book, I received a message from a man I remember writing for online. In fact, he had hired me to write several poems for a woman he was deeply in love with.

His story was hard to forget. His beloved came from a different background and had a long distance relationship. He was fully in love with this girl despite all of the obstacles in the way, and he wanted a poem created to make her feel seen and appreciated. He had written me to tell me the relationship didn't end up working out, but he still had a photo of the poem. He looked back upon it often, as it served as a reminder of a very special time in his life.

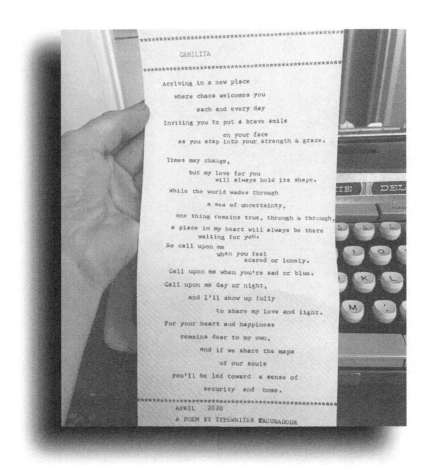

Sometimes our love stories aren't written the way we want them to be. And that's okay. At the end of the day, heartache and heartbreak can prepare us for the next level of love that is destined to come

after we do our work... As we heal, memories of lost love can remind us of the magic we are capable of sharing, and find a deeper appreciation for ourselves.

                    IN MEMORY OF
                THE LOVE OF MY LIFE
                    MY BELOVED
            VIRGINIA RAE

        My love for you will never
                    grow cold
            Not even in the dead of winter
                    When I brace myself
                        in the elements
            to watch others skate
                    on ice
                    as you once glided graceful
                            the champion
                        of my heart
                MY Love for you
                    is like a figure eight
                            It weaves
                    around my head
                            caught in infinity
        Oh how I miss you every day
                I cherish our memories
                    and see you in every
                            sunrise
                    and sunset
                for though you were too
                        precious for
                    this world
                        in physical
                            form
            I can now feel you everywhere
                a slight comfort to loss
        that   still ricochets my entire
                            mortal being
        by j.m brownlowe
                #typewritertroubadour
                    pdx, or
                    sept 8th, 2015

love the vice
        a poet could get drunk on
  the fierce visceral haunting love
              that can't be driven away from
                    no matter how many
            miles you put on a used car
                  the kind of love
          that twists the tongue
                and inspires one
          to jump against
                    walls
        spun out
    on street lamps
          scaring your heart
    and scarring your day dreams
              darkening
                  hearts and arrows
                    onto notebook
                        pages
          and soft wood
              because there is
      no one in this whole damn
                  world
          you'd rather be with

PART FIVE:

Inviting Love In

Poems for people's future lovers.
Poems to inspire self love.

Our final destination in Loveland is for the seekers, the dreamers, and all the lovers who haven't lost hope.

Celebrating second chances, new romances, and gratitude these poems reflect the stories of people who refuse to give up on finding lasting love and is dedicated to those who are doing the work to create space in their heart for another person.

Because at the end of the day — no matter how many times we have been hurt or felt unbearable loneliness, love is always the best medicine.

it is always about love
welcoming the power to
awaken all your senses —
for love is all around
in every sight and sound
taste and touch , open
your heart to receive
connection, where you will
be forgiven for any
imperfection, for love
knows patience and
tolerance -- how to heal
the deepest wounds, and
xxxtixfxxthexx   empower
you through the sensuality
of your soul.

by typewriter troubadour
    san diego, ca 2018
jeremy m brownlowe

connection

when we open our hearts
to another soul to
show up - safe and
authentic - we can
embrace our purpose
as human beings
for we are pack
animals who crave
connection
where love serves
as protection
from the XXXXXXXXX
illusion that we
are separate

by typewriter
troubadour

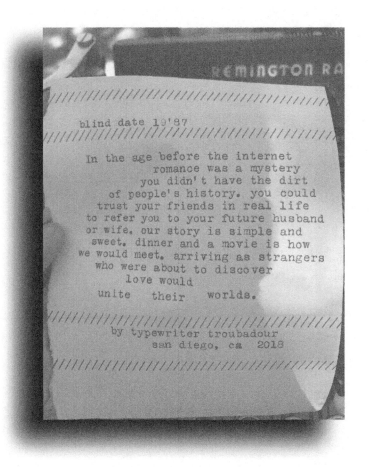

blind date 19'87

In the age before the internet
romance was a mystery
you didn't have the dirt
of people's history. you could
trust your friends in real life
to refer you to your future husband
or wife. our story is simple and
sweet. dinner and a movie is how
we would meet. arriving as strangers
who were about to discover
love would
unite   their   worlds.

by typewriter troubadour
san diego, ca 2018

Healing from Heartbreak
****

once i was broken
        unable to see past
    the scars you   left on my heart
            i felt my heart would never
        beat again
            quite the same
but one day
                I forced myself
    to let you go
                    so I could explore
who I had become
            get to know what I was
        passionate about
found out who my real friends were
        the ones who would stand by me
        and cheer me on
and now I realize
                            never scarred
        I was never broken
    just bruised
            and just like
    a temporary Mark on the skin
        the heartache you left me with
began to fade away

            typewritertroubadour

years have passed

    since we last saw each other

   during that time

     we lived seperate lives

   for destiny

wasn't ours to share

  our past

became distant memories

   we would revisit

    with a smile

  then destiny took a turn

   and guided each other

back onto the same path

 Our eyes lit up with excitement

our memories bright like the sun

of yesterday

   proving even though fate

   changed directions on us
there is always a map to retrace our steps
              back to
    the first time we fell

    in love

by jeremy m brownlowe

    typewritertroubadour

i am the awkward
        happy one,
    joyous and jovial

        i cannot conceal my interest
        in getting to know you
            more
                    my flame
        has Risen beyond a spark
            to light the way
                toward love.
///
by TYPEWRITER TROUBADOUR

            San diego, ca 2018

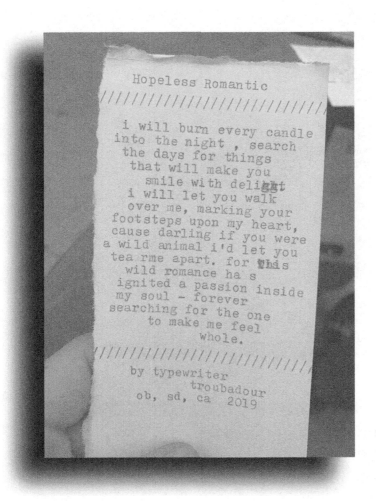

Hopeless Romantic
////////////////////////////////

i will burn every candle
into the night , search
the days for things
that will make you
smile with delight
i will let you walk
over me, marking your
footsteps upon my heart,
cause darling if you were
a wild animal i'd let you
tea rme apart. for this
wild romance ha s
ignited a passion inside
my soul - forever
searching for the one
to make me feel
whole.
////////////////////////////////

by typewriter
troubadour
ob, sd, ca 2019

DON QUIXOTE

chivalry
        surely isn't dead
                when shivers
            of romance
                  saunter
                    down the spines
                          of lovers
                the justice of the heart
                    sought by the
                            idealists
                                of amor
              to protect and defend
                    against
                  the wickedness
                          of humanity

by jeremy m brownlowe
        #typewritertroubadour
            pdx, or
                nov 2, 2015

FIRE SIGNS

SOMETIMES I WONDER
WHAT WOULD HAPPEN
IF WE LIT A MATCH
TO THIS COLD WEARY WORLD
AND WHAT WE WOULD BUILD
AFTER IT ALL WENT UP IN FLAMES.

                TYPEWRITER
                    TROUBADOUR

♥

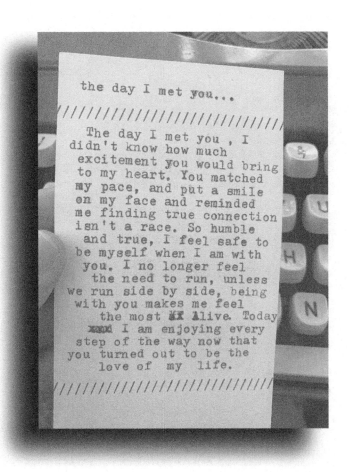

the day I met you...

////////////////////////////

The day I met you , I
didn't know how much
excitement you would bring
to my heart. You matched
my pace, and put a smile
on my face and reminded
me finding true connection
isn't a race. So humble
and true, I feel safe to
be myself when I am with
you. I no longer feel
the need to run, unless
we run side by side, being
with you makes me feel
the most XX Alive. Today
xxxx I am enjoying every
step of the way now that
you turned out to be the
love of my life.

////////////////////////////

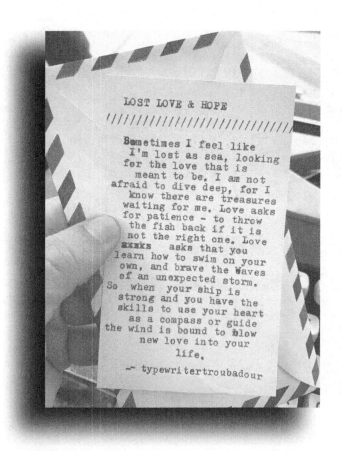

LOST LOVE & HOPE

//////////////////////////////////////

Sometimes I feel like
I'm lost as sea, looking
for the love that is
meant to be. I am not
afraid to dive deep, for I
know there are treasures
waiting for me. Love asks
for patience - to throw
the fish back if it is
not the right one. Love
xxxxx   asks that you
learn how to swim on your
own, and brave the waves
of an unexpected storm.
So when your ship is
strong and you have the
skills to use your heart
as a compass or guide
the wind is bound to blow
new love into your
life.

— typewritertroubadour

She wears her heart
      on her sleeve...
            literally...
      in fact - she spreads
       her love all over her body,
   a walking reminder
                that love is all
                      there is.
love is the medicine
          we need when our heart
      is sick, love is the magic
          number you call when
              you want to be kissed.
    Love -- she is like a queen
            of hearts,
    a living breathing work
          of art
    that inspires people to Sign
          their fate off to the stars.

V I V A   L A S   V E G A S   #25

TYPEWRITER // TROUBADOUR

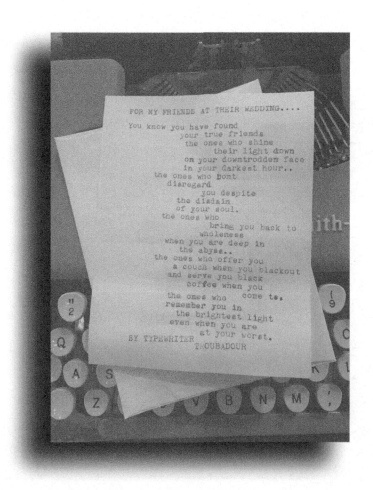

FOR MY FRIENDS AT THEIR WEDDING....

You know you have found
        your true friends
            the ones who shine
                their light down
            on your downtrodden face
            in your darkest hour..
    the ones who dont
        disregard
                you despite
            the disdain
        of your soul.
        the ones who
                bring you back to
                wholeness
        when you are deep in
            the abyss..
    the ones who offer you
        a couch when you blackout
        and serve you black
            coffee when you
        the ones who   come to.
        remember you in
            the brightest light
            even when you are
                at your worst.
        BY TYPEWRITER
                TROUBADOUR

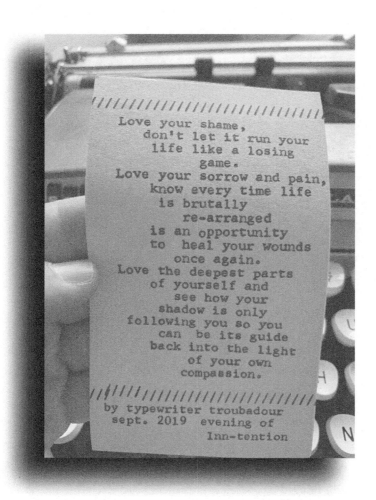

Love your shame,
don't let it run your
life like a losing
game.
Love your sorrow and pain,
know every time life
is brutally
re-arranged
is an opportunity
to heal your wounds
once again.
Love the deepest parts
of yourself and
see how your
shadow is only
following you so you
can be its guide
back into the light
of your own
compassion.

by typewriter troubadour
sept. 2019 evening of
Inn-tention

```
/////////////////////////////////////////////
    L O V E
/////////////////////////////////////////////

        searching for the feeling inside
        the one where we show our hearts
        fully , where we dare
         to celebrate another
            person's experience
            and embrace
          the greater good
          by learning to forgive.
     this journey starts inward
          it begins by looking
            in the mirror
         and giving up all fears
        that get in the way of love.


     -- typewriter troubadour

            san diego, ca

              sept. 2019 .


    //////////////////////////////////////////
```

```
************************************************

        My tongue is tangled
                trying to find the
                    right words
                to honor you,
        XXX you make me think
                    a little deeper
            diving into creativity ,
            for  ever since we met
                I see life
            a little different,
        and the more we share space
                and time,
        the more I expand my heart
                and my Mind.


        BY TYPEWRITER TROUBADOUR
        AUSTIN, TX
        OCTOBER 2021

************************************************
```

```
*******************************************

        BREAKING THE SPELL

*******************************************


        i'm breaking the spell
                you have over me
        breaking the chains
                you have tangled
                    around my heart
        walking away clean
                from your residue
            no longer tethered
                    to
                the past
            and stepping into
            AX    the power I
            earned by overcoming
        my  addiction  to   you.


    BY TYPEWRITER TROUBADOUR
    JOSHUA TREE MUSIC FEST 2021

*******************************************
```

Story Behind The Poem:

I don't know if the people I write for know that writing a poem to honor where they're at helps ME just as much as it helps them

— sometimes maybe even more!

This poem was written after I experienced a really hard breakup. It had been months since the relationship ended, but I still couldn't get this person out of my mind. Days were lost at sea, grieving what went wrong and what could have been. As someone who has addiction and codependency as part of their story, separating from this woman felt like a withdrawal from which I would never recover.

One of my favorite festivals to type at is The Joshua Tree Music Festival. It's a weekend of medicine for the soul in the Southern California desert full of great people, great music, and great healing.

This poem was written for a woman who had finally separated from a toxic partner. She was brave enough to share some of her story, and seemed to reflect what I had recently been through.

Maybe it was the magic of the desert or some sort of divine intervention, but after I wrote this poem I could feel the chains on my heart finally being released, finally ready to move forward.

I may be a simple man
                    but I want to give her all I can
        for I see the beauty
                    in a single rose
        picked just for her
                    It is my honor to serve
                        her as my queen
                to let her know with a whisper
                    how much she means to me
        I want to give her the kingdom
                    of her dreams
                    simply by giving her the keys
                    to my heart

        by jeremy m brownlowe
                            typewritertroubadour
                pdx, or   nov 2016

136

```
MAGIC   IN LOVE

****************************

    Love has the power
     to surprise you --
    how a single glance
    can ignite the power
   of a new romance. Love
      is magic - it can
     transform your soul,
       call back the pieces
      and make your heart
        feel whole. Love
        transcends all doubt
      and invites you to
       believe that anything
         is possible when
         you surrender and
    let   love   take the
              lead.

    by typewriter
          troubadour
   an evening of inn*tention
```

POLYAMOROUS LOVE

The human heart is so big
        it explodes
     in all directions
        seeking a special
        kind of connection
        with self
          with a lover
             with a partner
        though it isn't based purely
           on fable
too much pressure
           on one person
               can be a killjoy
        but rather
            honoring what each
     person has to give
           without comparison
             and hopefully
             with communication
           as open
               as the arms
          we stretch
             to embrace
          all who we adore

        by jeremy m brownlowe
          typewriter troubadour
          pdx, or
             may 2016

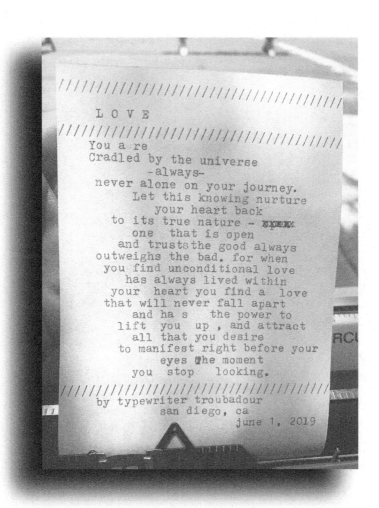

L O V E

You a re
Cradled by the universe
        -always-
never alone on your journey.
    Let this knowing nurture
        your heart back
    to its true nature - ~~nyexx~~
        one that is open
    and trusts the good always
outweighs the bad. for when
you find unconditional love
    has always lived within
    your heart you find a love
    that will never fall apart
        and ha s   the power to
    lift you up , and attract
        all that you desire
    to manifest right before your
        eyes the moment
        you stop looking.

by typewriter troubadour
        san diego, ca
                june 1, 2019

//

LOVE YOU BIG AS SKY
//

The horizon reminds me
there is a thin blue line
between you and me , and
        what a glory to see
your true colors come alive
with each sunset and
        sunrise. Love like
ours is forever infinite -
where all of the stars
answer with wishes.
        I love you
like the sea loves the
tide. When I think of you
my heart opens wide
I want to shout your name
across the country side
        cradled by your love
        under a big blue sky.
//
By typewriter Troubadour
        san diego, ca
                july 2019

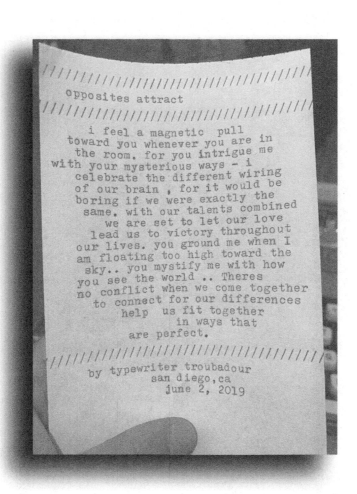

opposites attract

i feel a magnetic pull
toward you whenever you are in
the room. for you intrigue me
with your mysterious ways - i
celebrate the different wiring
of our brain , for it would be
boring if we were exactly the
same. with our talents combined
we are set to let our love
lead us to victory throughout
our lives. you ground me when I
am floating too high toward the
sky.. you mystify me with how
you see the world .. Theres
no conflict when we come together
to connect for our differences
help us fit together
in ways that
are perfect.

by typewriter troubadour
san diego, ca
june 2, 2019

MODERN ROMANCE

by typewriter
troubadour

6.10.17/sd,ca

craving connection

we search... worldwide

with a swipe
    of a finger
        on a hand
            that really just
                wants
                    to be held
call me old fashioned
    but 1 would rather discover
    a new lover
    anyplace other than while
        I am sitting on a toilet

maybe a park, a show, a train or
        even a plane or bizarre
        form of happenstance

                    modern
        but no -- the tragedy is
people are already enamoured with
the future, the possibility of a
new match, that they miss out on
        the people who are
        right b e f o r e their eyes

MISS YOU

****

Baby, I miss you
when the cold winds blow
I miss you more than
    you know.. Cause
    when we're together
      it's hard to
          let you go.
  Truth be told,
        The moment I met
      you was the moment
          I was sold.
 Baby, I miss you, and
    I know you can't rush
        fate, and I know
      your love is well
          worth the wait.

BY TYPEWRITER TROUBADOUR
FOR MAGGIE
ROCKABILLAQUE 2021

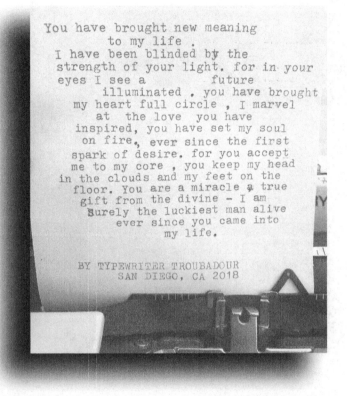

You have brought new meaning
        to my life .
 I have been blinded by the
 strength of your light. for in your
 eyes I see a   future
        illuminated . you have brought
 my heart full circle , I marvel
        at the love you have
 inspired, you have set my soul
        on fire, ever since the first
 spark of desire. for you accept
 me to my core , you keep my head
 in the clouds and my feet on the
 floor. You are a miracle a true
 gift from the divine - I am
        Surely the luckiest man alive
        ever since you came into
                my life.

        BY TYPEWRITER TROUBADOUR
           SAN DIEGO, CA 2018

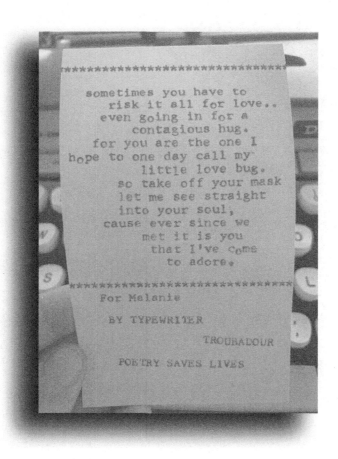

****
sometimes you have to
risk it all for love..
even going in for a
contagious hug.
for you are the one I
hope to one day call my
little love bug.
so take off your mask
let me see straight
into your soul,
cause ever since we
met it is you
that I've come
to adore.
****
For Melanie
BY TYPEWRITER
TROUBADOUR
POETRY SAVES LIVES

where down the line
did you forget
to love
and be loved
is your birth right
ever since you were born
into this fabulous form..

the caged bird sings
itself
to sleep
         while weary
              wolves
    howl at a lonesome
              m o o n .
     As
        we silly humans
spend our time
wondering
if our souls
are part of the pack
or a life of solitude.
✶✶✶✶✶✶✶✶✶✶✶✶✶✶✶✶✶✶✶✶✶✶✶✶✶✶✶✶✶✶
    XXXXX JUNE 2020 XXX

XXX

```
You are my spirit mate
            the man whom was patient
                        enough to wait
        for me to come back around
                after burying myself
                    underground
            when the storm sets in
    It is an old habit
                to retreat
                        into the depths
            of my own soul
                    but rest assured
            with you
                    I am learning
                            to become
                                    whole
        as we grow together
            we must learn
                    to loosen
                        our tether
                on each other
    to allow
            is to love
                    is to know
                            the in's
                                and the outs
        of the cycle of  our bond
                    trusting we
                        will always
                            remain fond
            no matter what
                    is going on
        in our personal  routes
                to fullfillment
```

SOUL MATE

Before I knew you
            in the physical realm
                 I could sense your aura
        burning in the dark
                        trying to signal
                 me
        to your heart beat
            my twin flame
                        how you warm me
            the soul screams
                     for companionship
            to make two halves a whole
                    I have been waiting
                        my whole life for you
        yet when I meet you
                I feel as if I
                        have known you
                 for eons

        byxsmbxxmxxxx
                 by jeremy m. brownlowe
                                    aug 6, 2015
                 pdx, or
            #typewritertroubadour

148

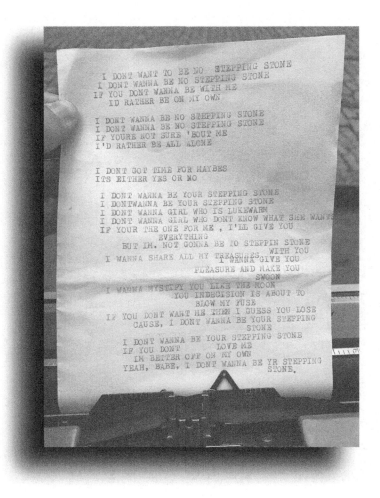

                    ROBBIE   &   FABI
****

            Even in the dark bar
                I knew you would
                light up my stars
            For your smile burned bright
                like candle light.
            Maybe it was the booze,
                but something told me
            I had to say hello
                to you.
            Now we are engaged
                a nd life is changed
                for the better
            for when you find true love
                nothing else matters.

            by typewriter troubadour
                charleston, sc

                nov 2021

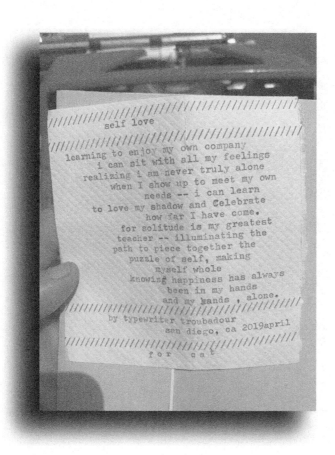

self love

learning to enjoy my own company
i can sit with all my feelings
realizing i am never truly alone
when I show up to meet my own
needs -- i can learn
to love my shadow and Celebrate
how far I have come.
for solitude is my greatest
teacher -- illuminating the
path to piece together the
puzzle of self, making
myself whole
knowing happiness has always
been in my hands
and my hands , alone.

by typewriter troubadour
san diego, ca 2019april

for cat

```
************************************************

        THE RIGHT PERSON
************************************************

    I AM SEARCHING FOR THE RIGHT
        PERSON FOR ME, FOR THERE ARE
              MANY FISH IN THE SEA
          BUT A LOT OF THEM STINK.
    I WANT SOMEONE WHO WANTS TO
                  DIVE DEEP
          SOMEONE WHO DOESNT FREAK
              OUT AT THE NEXT
        LEVEL OF INTIMACY.
    I HOPE TO MANIFEST ALL OF
          MY DREAMS
        AND CELEBRATE THE ONES
          OF THE PERSON WHO GETS
                WITH ME.
    FOR I HAVE DONE THE WORK
          LEARNING TO LOVE
        MYSELF UNCONDITIONALLY
        AND IM NOT GONNA BE
        MESSIN WITH ANY MORE
        FOOLS OR TRICKERY, AND
        HOLD OUT FOR THE RIGHT

          PERSON   WHO LIVES
              WITH   INTEGRITY.
```

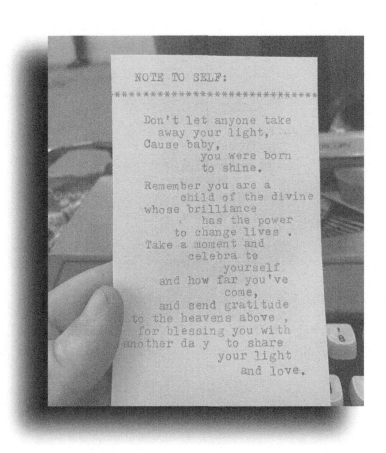

NOTE TO SELF:
****

Don't let anyone take
away your light,
Cause baby,
you were born
to shine.

Remember you are a
child of the divine
whose brilliance
has the power
to change lives .
Take a moment and
celebra te
yourself
and how far you've
come,
and send gratitude
to the heavens above ,
for blessing you with
another da y to share
your light
and love.

POEMS
FOR
OTHER
PEOPLE'S
LOVERS

Thank you to everyone who was open to sharing their story to inspire these poems.

Thank you to friends, family, lovers, and God for showing me the love & support when I needed it most.

Love Conquers All.
Love is Medicine.
Love Saves Lives.

Other Titles by Typewriter Troubadour:

Select Poems (2015-2018):
Poetry On Various Topics,
For Various People,
In Various Places.

Poetry Saves Lives (2020)

The Adventures Of
Typewriter Troubadour
(J.M. Browne, 2020)

Order Online:
www.typewritertroubadour.com

Jeremy M. Brownlowe is the man behind Typewriter Troubadour. Since 2015, Jeremy has been creating custom poems for people in public places. When he is not driving town to town, living out of his camper van, he splits his time between Southern California and North Georgia. In addition to his work as Typewriter Troubadour, Jeremy has published many works under the pen name, J.M. Browne. When he is not writing on the road Jeremy enjoys baths, collecting crystals, and making music. He is always ready for the next story.

Made in the USA
Monee, IL
07 April 2022

93542304R00090